Workable Words

Deep Words For Simple Living

Workable Words

Deep Words For Simple Living

By

Sterlin Sookoo

authorHOUSE®

You may ask by viewing the title of this book what are workable words? Well simply they are communicated principles that one can put to work or use in one's life. In life we encounter either words that are workable or words that are unworkable (which are words that will not work for us and bear no advantage or benefit to our lives). This book is dedicated to arming you with words that one can gain benefit from when one allows such words to be involved in the realm of everyday living. First and foremost we must define the three grounds upon which our lives rest. I have divided up our lives based on these three grounds and these include (1) our internal or inside life which we can also call our "contained life" (2) our middle life which we can also call our "central life" and (3) our external or outside life which we can call our "circumference life." Each one of these grounds of life will be explained as we go along in the book and for each ground of our living we shall apply words that we can all use for each ground or realm of living. For simpler analysis we can view each ground of our life in chart form!

Our Inside Life or (Contained Life)
Our Middle Life or (Central Life)
Our Outside Life or (Circumference Life)

Let us now begin our journey with the unfolding of these workable words that will work to produce for us a life that is worthy of wonderful living in a masterfully made design!

The Internal or "Contained" Life

Our Internal/Inside or Contained Life is that part of our lives that is contained within the shell or envelope of our physical bodies or frame. It is those internal thought processes, motivations and emotions that only the individual is well acquainted with within. It is the unseen world shielded from outside eyes but only seen by the eyes of each individual who looks within themselves daily!

Workable Word #1

"Real Living is always an Internal Reality"

Working These Words: If there is one question that should govern the minds of men should be the question: What really is real living about? For some it is pleasure and for others it involves possessions and then for several more real living is about pursuits or even finding the right people! However with the above workable word real living is internal in its reality which means that one can have pleasures, possessions, pursuits and even people but still not have an internal peaceful reality within. Pleasures, pursuits, possessions and people last only a lifetime and no one is guaranteed how long that the time of one's lifetime actually will be but even if one had not acquired any of these items of life but had a state of calm restful assurance within then one has truly then attained what real living is all about! We must always remember this that the man who dies with a smile and has nothing is always better than a man who has everything and dies without one. In death we take nothing from this life with us except the real peace we had within which can eventually be translated over into our last dying smile!

Workable Word #2

"A Life lifted within is a life worthy of living"

Working These Words: According to this workable word we can see what a worthy life is all about! Worthy living or living a life of true meaning and worth is about being lifted up within. In encounters in this life one may experience "put downs" in one way or another either from persons or problems! However if one within maintains an upward or uplifted attitude it matters not what tries to put own down. There is that beneficial internal motivation that decisively boosts one with the energizing power and ability to determine within to reach back to the top again. Though outwardly the view of life at present is downward but inwardly a richer view of life is that soon one's life will return upward again. It matters not then the "let down" moments in one's outside life but the "lifted up" motivation one has from a life that is lived within. This beautiful angle of living will eventually achieve the blessing of a worthy life!

Workable Word #3

"A Sure Status is Always a Solid Self"

Working These Words: In this our third workable word we shall develop the idea of status. Status is seen as the position or standing of a person. The above workable word tells us what a sure position or standing is in life. A sure position for life is to be a solid person in life. Life at times can break us into many fragmented pieces but over the step by step process of time we can reconnect each broken piece and return it back to its original position and become a complete solid person again!. Remember the possession of self-obtained material substance cannot compare with the possession of a solid mature self because one can lose material substance but a mature solid self can work to recover at times the substance that has been lost! In being realistic I will admit that certain broken pieces cannot at times be replaced like the loss of a loved one or a divorce in a marital relationship but operating with a solid self means learning the art of remaining unbroken in the midst of many things that are trying to break one apart!

Workable Word #4

"Our Free Flowing Determines Our Full Going"

Working These Words: This workable word teaches us that how well one flows in life determines how well one goes in their life. Life many times is about flow. Flow refers to the movement of a particular object from one destination to another destination. In life we can periodically experience blockages to our flow and thus we can come to a standstill in our progressive movement onwards to a better place. However external flow that may be blocked can be revived by internal flow that is unblocked. The strong inward flow of motivation that we have within can be stirred up within us till it flows out of us in sturdy constructive action that strongly pushes away the blockage that has hindered our external flow in life!

Workable Word #5

"Our plug-ins produces our passions"

Working These Words: The above workable word declares to us that what we partner with or are plugged into produces the passions that proceed out of us! A passion is a goal blended with one's affection. The partnership we have with what we are plugged into always produces our passions that we will eventually promote. Caution therefore must be exercised in our participations so that our passions will always be pure. Impure passions are a direct result of impure participations and hence why the impure always produces the illegal or the illicit. Ensuring one is always guided by pure passions will also ensure that one will prevail and see oneself productively promoted!

Workable Word #6

"Advancement within Loneliness is greater than addiction to Loneliness"

Working These Words: This next workable word deals with loneliness. With loneliness there is a loss of significance and satisfaction with one's self which may stem from the lack of companionship or a sense of lingering isolation from others. Loneliness becomes an addiction rather than a place for future advancement. Many become addicted to its sadness rather than advance with its strategy. Loneliness must be seen as a birthing chamber for the strategic and not a bowing down to sorrow! In loneliness a much larger place exists as it can be the launching pad into greater levels of liberty such as new locations or newer aspects of learning that before we may have never had.

Workable Word #7

"Intense certainty is our internal concrete"

Working These Words: This meaningful workable word that can be comprehended truly has great merit with it because it speaks to us about certainty. Certainty is the effective internal assurance that guides us through the elements of external adversity. In our internal core it can become an incorruptible concrete. Though the cracks of uncertainty may appear on the outside we know that within the concrete of certainty will not crack! Certainty is therefore that solid ingredient in our inward lives that stabilizes us so that when our outward lives are shaken by confusion inwardly we will not collapse but still securely stand.

Workable Word #8

"Memory matures motivated momentum"

Working these Words: With this workable word we see that memory is like fertilizer to the force of momentum. The more positive additions that are made by this essential element the more positive growth is given over to our momentum. Momentum involves the continuous movement of a specific object that is related in the context of speed. The productive speed of our momentum is therefore dependent upon the supply of productive memories that we may have. Productive or Positive memories are therefore the fuel that allow us to have faster momentum that can move us past the madness that externally tries to forcefully prevail over us.

Workable Word #9

"Inside speeches silences outside sounds"

Working these Words: Here we see with this important workable word that our inside speeches puts to silence the sounds that are outside! We have many outside sounds that compete with the speeches that we have within. Many of these "sounds" come from sources that have set into our lives tension and suffering. However the value of our own speech within will subdue these victimizing sounds that are without. As our internal "speakings" of value grow within us they influence away those external sounds of victimization that try to grab hold of us. They are therefore the silencer that subdues those sounds of suffering that seemingly scream at us!

Workable Word #10

"The watered soul soothes all worthless stings"

Working These Words: This workable word of worth shows us the worthy value of having a watered soul. In life our sufferings can come from the stings of many struggles that have brought much sorrow to us. The soul that is watered today will heal itself from the stings that it faces tomorrow. We must water ourselves with the water of worth so that the stings of worthlessness are all washed away. Watering ourselves with such wisdom will wipe away many of these worthless woes that have worked themselves inside of us in an attempt to weary us and eventually wreck us but because of how well we have been watered with the wisdom of our own worth we are now well conditioned to not want these woes anymore.

Workable Word #11

"The storagehouse reveals the storagekeeper"

Working These Words: Here we see from this workable word that the house of storage that we have is a revelation of the keeper of that storage! The contents that one has stored away inside of them reveal the character of themselves as a storer because that which is displayed on the outside demonstrates all that we have put as deposits within. Therefore it is imperative that we store inside those successful items which will indwell us and initiate us into that which we can later on be impressively satisfied with. These items are those we have internalized that can lead us towards a more in-depth influence over our present issues. It is therefore to be well noted that the type of total deposits that we have deposited determines the type of depositor that we are!

Workable Word #12

"Burning brightness banishes the blanket of blackness"

Working These Words: What a wonderful workable word to witness! The brightness that burns within us is able to banish away every black blanket placed upon us! Many times the black blanket of burdens can cover us with bleakness but the burning bright flame we have within us can be lit so brightly on the inside that it burns away the fog that comes from the blackness of bleakness. The shining of our brightness can bring into submission all that may try to blacken our lives and make it bittersweet. Thus the more we burn in a brighter way within will be the more that we burn out of us every blemish that has been put in us by bleakness which tries to blacken our behavior so that we will behave as though we are always to be broken and beaten down but thankfully the brightness that we burn with within tells us otherwise.

Workable Word #13

"A healed core is medicine to harassing sores"

Working these Words: In this workable word that works healing into our lives we see that the healing substance that we have internally can be medicine to the harassing sores that we have externally! Once our core is filled with healing then there will be a pouring out of that internal healing upon our external sores that have harassed us so that they might eventually be cured. These sores may have come from a series of outward interactions but a cured core can create an inward outpouring of the contents of that cure that we have within that can overwhelm us outwardly to such a degree that result in us being made cured from these sores that we have on the outside in the same way that we are already cured from them within so that how we are on the outside matches with how we are on the inside!

Workable Word #14

"Complete control contradicts counteractive challenges"

Working these Words: Control which is the ability within oneself to remain stable can counter those elemental challenges that attempt to persuade us into being unstable! Internal control is therefore an opposing force to the opposition we face from counteractive challenges! These counteractive challenges try to make us uncontrolled but when we operate with complete control we can obtain complete calmness to be able to undo all that might be counteractive and counterproductive against us. Complete control therefore can allow us catch hold of a clear composure that can counter all counterattacks that may attempt to completely crush us!

Workable Word #15

"The silent identity dethrones the skilful insulter"

Working these Words: This is a powerful workable word that we should productively work into our lives. The identity that is unknown to others will overthrow the insults that others may think that they know about us! Our silent identity involves our unrevealed self and it contains our secretly unseen influence and importance. No matter how skilled someone may be at insulting us once we are sure within ourselves about our secret importance which has not been seen in their sight then we can win over the impediment of insults that they are trying to invade our internal selves with. The knowledge of our importance diminishes insults that are used by others in an attempt to knock us down and such knowledge cause us to know that the indignity suffered from insults that we have been inflicted with can always be defeated by involving ourselves with our influence and how much more influential we can be instead.

Workable Word #16

"Self friendships counters society's forsaking"

Working These Words: There are many times that we may think that the loss of friendships means that we are at loss with the familiar. It is therefore important that at that moment in time that we become forsaken that we establish a new found friendship which is the friendship of self. True friendship with self is not a friendship with selfishness but rather it is a friendship with self supportiveness. Self friendship therefore is demonstrating support for ourselves when there is absolutely no one there to support us. It is in those moments of time when we have no friends around that our best friend can be found in a meaningfulness of who we actually are truly being manifested to our own selves.

Workable Word #17

"Potential Produces Potency"

Working These Words: Potential is the ability to develop when opportunity is available whereas potency is developed power needed for opportunities that come later on. Potential that is used by us can help develop power that later on can become useful to us. To move into future power it begins with moving into our present potential. Potency or power is therefore a product of potential that is being productively pursued. Therefore in the pursuit of potency there must be the polishing of our potential. A well polished potential always can produce a well founded and well grounded potency!

Workable Word #18

"A pure infection cleanses us from the perverseness of incidents"

Working These Words: There are times we may be infected by the impure from incidents that we have involved ourselves with but there is a greater "infection' to become "infected" with so to speak and that involves becoming "infected" with the pure instead of the impure! An infection involves the impartation or infusion of that which attempts to internally implant itself in us! Once we become "infected" with that which is pure it will immunize us from incidents that may attempt to pervert us or make us impure. Pure "infections" involves the positioning or placement of a persuasion that tells us to push ourselves away that which will try pervert us or make us impure and instead propel, prompt or push ourselves toward us that which is pure!

Workable Word #19

"Released Resources Resists Restrictions"

Working These Words: Here is another powerful workable word which declares to us about the resources that are released in us because that which is released in us can be released from us to resist the restrictions that obstruct us. Internal resources are the inward wealth that we contain within that make us rich on the inside. The richness we have internally can produce inside of us an undying refusal to allow restrictions of any kind to rule over us. It is therefore important to our internal world that we rely upon the resources that we have released within for out from them comes our resistance against all restraining influences.

Workable Word #20

"The thread called turning ties us down when turmoil tries to take us into tragedy"

Working These Words: A thread may be seen as a twine for tying. There is a thread that we need to weave our lives with when turmoil tries to trouble us and it is thread called turning. This thread will tie us down with inward security when the outward storms of trouble blow upon us with its breath! Turning indicates a time of transformation in spite of the terribleness of a trial. Turning tells us within that though an issue may be troubling in time it can transform itself into that which is tasteful later on in its totality. Thus when turmoil threatens to tear us apart this thread of turning can take hold of us with the trustworthy truth that though turmoil may be trying to take us into tragedy things can eventually turn for us in a much more terrific way!

Workable Words #21

"The seat called self commitment can be a seat of security"

Working These Words: There is a seat worthy of us sitting in that promises us much security and it is the seat of self commitment. Self commitment involves connecting with the service to oneself. Many times we are involved in the service to others at the neglect of service to self. Self commitment therefore specifies commitment to my own self in the equal proportion of being committed to others who are unlike my own self. To sit in the seat of self commitment means also that I am sitting in the secure seat of being in service to me even when others are so self centered and may never ever be of any service to me. I learn to always be connected with me even when others are disconnected from me.

Workable Words #22

"Our pourings form our principles"

Working These Words: Here now is another important workable word of consequence that we should also take note of which indicates to us that what is poured into us forms in us the principles that controls our life. A pouring is a particular investment that we have permitted. The interior principles we operate in today were due to the exterior pourings that we allowed into internal world in our yesterday. If a principle fails to productively perform for us then we must empty ourselves of that which has been originally poured into us. To obtain a new productive principle that will cause us to eventually prevail we must get under a new pouring that can pilot our lives into a new place.

Workable Words #23

"Our air quality determines our acceleration"

Working These Words: Air quality deals with the quality of the surrounding atmosphere. Internally in our inside life we have a particular "air" quality or atmospheric quality that we have to maintain! Air contains the elemental gas oxygen that once burnt or used by a particular body produces the acceleration of the said body. The quality of acceleration is determined by the quantity of the air's oxygen and so too it is with our internal life when it comes to our inside atmosphere. Once our interior life's atmosphere is enriched with an enriching element then we will everyday be energized with external acceleration. We can only accelerate as far as we want based upon the aspects we allow functioning in our internal life's atmosphere!

Workable Words #24

"The inner building can involve us in the best"

Working These Words: Here also is yet another important word and that is that the building built within can bring us to the best that we are worthy of being brought into. In our interior life we must build a building that is built with bricks that contain in them the best. Once we build internally with the best then we will breakthrough externally into the best. We must fill this building with the best beliefs, behavior, and brilliance that will boost us into the most beautiful blessing than what we have ever had before. Our building must therefore contain only those beneficial bricks that once built with build us up into that which will be only of absolute beauty!

Workable Words #25

"Meaning triumphs over mournings"

Working These Words: This workable word is vital in our lives since it reveals our victory. Meaning is the intended motivation that controls our lives that enables us to triumph over our individual mournings. We need to invest ourselves in intentional motivation that is found at the core of our internal existence and when such an investment by ourselves is made then we are actually intentionally creating for ourselves meaningful and important impact that overcomes mourning. Though we may mourn now once we have attained our life's meaningfulness we are able to navigate ourselves beyond the mourning of the now and enter into the manifestation of the new!

Workable Words #26

"Our windows determine our weather"

Working These Words: Windows are openings that create an entry point to allow outside factors to enter into our world. In the natural environment they allow the external weather to invade our normal existence. In our internal life's environment we also have windows which are our eyes and ears. These windows open us up to the working elements of the outside weather conditions which can be the worse weather conditions at times. These sometimes work their way within us and it is those times when these worse weather conditions are allowed to work within us that we must learn to close our windows and only open them to weather conditions that will only let in the wonderful on the inside of us!

Workable Words #27

"Walls prevent waverings"

Working These Words: Walls are solid blocks that can act as solid barriers against shakings that waverings can bring. To waver means to sway to and fro. In our inward life to the degree that our walls are solid to that degree will we be prevented from wavering or swaying or swinging from side to side and therefore this will determine how well we remain solidly secure on the inside. When we waver it is because we are at war within ourselves because we are unsure as to which way will lead us into that which will be worthwhile for our lives and away from worthless wastage. The solid walls of wisdom will act as a shield against the shaky waverings of worry and strong walls of worth will become a shelter from the winds of worthlessness.

Workable Words #28

"Worthy identification is our ink within"

Working These Words: This workable word is truly worthy of our consideration because it speaks about worthy identification. According to this workable word identification can be compared to ink. Ink is a substance that stains upon impact and so too we must allow ourselves to be impacted with the importance of having a worthy identity of integrity. It is with the ink of integrity in identity that we are able to write out the image design for our lives that we can later on inherit. It therefore matters not if others have impacted us with inferiority because once we are much more greatly impacted and imprinted with the worth of our identity then we will not involve ourselves with any inaccuracies that may be about us that either may try to impede us or interfere with us.

Workable Words #29

"The cleansing agent of cleverness clears up the criticisms of cursings"

Working These Words: Here is another powerful workable word since it teaches us that we can fill our internal lives with the cleansing agent of cleverness! This cleansing agent called cleverness is able to clear away the corrupting stains we may have encountered from the negative criticisms that we have been cursed with! Every time we are negatively criticized we realize that we have more cleverness than the critic who is trying to curse us with their critical attitude! We must therefore regularly cleanse ourselves with this detergent so that we may liberate ourselves from the deterioration brought upon us by the words used by others who attempt to lay curses upon us so that they will eventually detour us. Therefore when we use this fresh detergent it will cleanse us from future detours that others have set for us.

Workable Words #30

"A capable character is our comfortable cushion"

Working These Words: Here in this workable word we learn that a comfortable cushion to rest upon is a capable character that should be constant with us. A cushion is a soft pad that is able to soften the strikes that may be made by continuous blows. When our character possesses the capability of a cushion then our character is more than able to absorb any crushing blows that may be caused by others in an attempt to cause us to crumble! Therefore with our character like that of a cushion we demonstrate that we are able to convert every form of chaotic conflict into that which we can use both awesomely in a creative and in a colorful way!

The Middle or "Central" Life

Our Middle or Central Life is that location found in our lives where we believe movement is an impossibility. Helplessness and Hopeless usually finds its way in this middle zone. It is the place that we have arrived at where the important decisions concerning which appropriate targets in life to turn our attention towards must be made so that we may transfer ourselves out of the middle and transform ourselves into an eventual masterpiece.

Workable Words #31

"Misery melts down the initiative of the soul in the middle"

Working These Words: Misery involves the discomfort of discontentment and disappointment. It can be like a melting fire that melts down the moving force of initiative inside of our souls. Initiative is that moving energy on the inside of us that has been ignited within us to move us beyond the middle stage of life. Misery must not be allowed to melt away any attempts that we may make to move into that which can be momentous for our life. When the melting fires of misery burn we must add the fresh cooling agent of favorable initiative to put out its flame because initiative will aid in fanning away all that this machine called misery will try to force upon us!

Workable Words #32

"Constructive thought constructs the correct"

Working These Words: Constructive thought is thinking that puts together the blocks of correct calculations that later on builds itself up into creativity! In this middle part of life we must have that mental activity that manufactures that which can bring mending to our lives. Constructive thought therefore contains that mental activity that calculates all of the correct constructions that will be needed so as to construct our way through the mass of confusion that may cloud our way. The more correct constructions that are able to construct then the more content we are able to add to our creativity. Correct constructions can include cooperating with others, cheerfulness that incorporates optimism and conduct that can cause us to be involved later on in creative opportunities. With these outgrowths of constructive thought we are able to cement ourselves in the correct operation of our life.

Workable Words #33

"Self support can be one's sweetest support"

Working These Words: In this central area of our lives that we come to we many times search for those supporters who will be like sweeteners who are able to add sweetness to the sourness of our life by supporting us and it is by the sweetness of their support that we believe that we are able to change our present sourness into something much more substantial. However there are times when such support from others is nonexistent and it is therefore in those moments that support from oneself must become even more existent in our lives. This is where the support of ourselves must occur so that we will not succumb to any obstacles which try to oppose us! When we support ourselves when no support from others is given we are able to saturate ourselves with the solace of a sound mind that we are more than able to see solution to our situations.

Workable Words #34

"Pushing power is proportional to the force of passion"

Working These Words: Pushing power is the power that one must exercise to push away that which has been pushed against oneself. In the middle place we face many issues that push themselves on us and therefore we must develop the ability to throw back that which has been thrown on us. The force of our pushing is dependent upon the force of our passion. To the degree that our passion is forceful to that degree will our push be forceful as well. Never must we let that which sticks us in the middle place subdue us there. Therefore with all the exertion that must be exercised we must apply essential pressure of our own personal pushing power to push away with all passionate force from within us all that presses against us that attempts to prevent us from eventually fulfilling our life's purpose.

Workable Words #35

"A doorway mindset can setup our deliverance"

Working These Words: This workable word truly needs to be worked into our lives. In this central part of life that we come to we may be faced with denial. Denial is a mindset that tells us the doors in our life is locked. With this workable word we learn that we need to change our mindsets from one that sees a door that is locked to one that sees an open doorway! With a mind that only sees a door from every kind of discouragement or deterrence then this means that we are setting up ourselves to be delivered from the middle place rather than thinking that our lives are being delivered over to disaster.

Workable Words #36

"The measure of our feeding determines the movement of us forward"

Working These Words: Here again we see a workable word of worth that is worthy of the weight of our lives resting upon it. It tells us that the amount of what we feed upon determines our forward moving activity! Forward movement is a direct result of regular feedings which eventually produces for us the "feet" necessary to advance towards the front in a fast pace. We must therefore find those items that we can deem as our necessary food whereby we may feed upon such items and gain the propulsion to go forward. Our food must consist of fresh imaginations that see us going far away from the middle that we have presently found ourselves in to the point where we will eventually gain a life that is once again fully fit and fully functioning.

Workable Words #37

"A crossroads is a vertical road and a horizontal road coming together"

Working These Words: A crossroads is the joining together of two roadways that are in opposite direction with each other and do not seem to conform to each other! When we look at a crossroad from a side view we see an X shape but when we look at a crossroad from an above view we can tilt the crossroad and see a T shape instead. When in the middle ground of our existence we come to a crossroad we tend to see an X shape that indicates cancellation for us but we must change our view so that we can instead see a T-shape that indicates transformation. Our view of our crossroad determines our victory over its captivity over us. When our vision of our crossroads is changed then the view of our conquering capability over our crossroads will become complete!

Workable Words #38

"Idea making moves away idleness"

Working These Words: Idea making is the creative ability to manufacture ideas that will carry us away from idle ways. Idleness involves inactivity. The major imbalance that keeps us in the middle is inactivity because it can keep us away from marked involvement in that which can impart into us important motivation. However the continuous making of ideas helps maneuver us out of idleness and into being industrious so that we will be able to make for our ownselves with the implementation of important ideas an improved life! Thus idea making can cause us to make possible our own measurable increase since it is more than capable of inverting idleness into inventiveness!

Workable Words #40

"The calm in the middle can become the cutting edge of the magnificent"

Working These Words: In the central part of life it can appear to be absolutely calm where it seems that things have cooled off for us. At one time it seemed that life with us was lively but now in the middle life around us is more lethargic. However it is in these sessions of cooling off times that we are more able to concentrate on those tactics that we can use like the cutting edge of a surgeon's scalpel to cut through our turmoils and our troubles. A sharp cutting edge is many times able to cut through the most stubborn of substances and we must therefore allow ourselves in these moments of "silence" in the middle to be sharpened like that of a scalpel so that when these mome of "silence" try to seal us in we can slice through its sea something that is more magnificent than that which tries us in.

Workable Words #39

"The nothing of the preser can become the something of our potential"

Working These Words: In the present we at times
nothing when we are in the paralysis of the middle
times where our present state seems to be filled with n
must pursue that which is necessary so that such a pι
develop later on into substantial and stable potential.
is that practice that produces the profitable out of the
and the productive out of that which to others may see
pointless. Therefore we must not concern ourselves
emptiness that may be in our present today but we mι
into that emptiness profitable and productive potential
enable us to push ourselves out of emptiness and into
more enjoyable and energized place!

Workable Words #41

"Drown not yourself in dread but drown yourself in your destination"

Working These Words: There are times when our dread seems like it is drowning us but there is of course a better substance that we should instead drown ourselves in and it is our destination. There are two kinds of consciousness that are conclusively described in the workable word that has been declared for us above and these involve the consciousness that facilitates dread and the consciousness that facilitates a destination. Dread consciousness involves being terrified of the future whereas destination consciousness involves a taking hold of the future. Whenever we are faced with dread we should defeat it with the desire for our future desirable destination which will help direct us out of the fearfulness of dread and into a fabulous destiny!

Workable Words #42

"The dark of the night never substitutes the mark of delight"

Working These Words: Here again is a powerfully practical workable word that we can apply into the middle area of our lives. In this central life zone we can be confronted with dark moments that consequently may be dark as the night. We must however concern ourselves with another moment while we are mindful of our time in the middle and that moment is the one later on that brings major and majestic delight. No matter the lifeless night time of darkness our lives may be in now that which is next in line for us we must learn to look forward to and this is the new time of delight that is able to launch us into a much more far reaching liberty further than the lamentation that is in our now!

Workable Words #43

"The shifter tops the stayer"

Working These Words: There are two groups of people we can define in this workable word and they are the shifter and the stayer! The stayer is the one who remains in their current setting whereas the shifter is the one who changes the context of their surroundings. We are either one or the other in this central character of our life which we have now come to. The stayer stays below while the shifter stands on top and in the middle of life the merits of being up should be sought beyond the mistake of being under. Once we shift ourselves beyond staying where we are we will shift ourselves into standing in the area that we have a right to ascend to.

Workable Words #44

"The unchangeable now is not always unadjustable later"

Working These Words: We are faced in the middle of our existence with that which seems to be unchangeable and we may believe that such cannot be fixed. However on many occasions that which may seem obstinate to change can later on be found to have within it the opportunity for change. The situation with the unchangeable is that it can at times touch upon that which has seemingly settled down itself as "permanent" in our lives and such can be a constant factor that one has a tendency to presently face in this central area of life! However that which seems to be unchangeable does not necessarily mean that it has to remain in an unfixable, unalterable or unadjustable state! Considering this then the force of our approach must be one that takes that which appears as if it cannot be changed and with the conviction to see change attend to our circumstances with full concentrated attention so that we will see change come to what seems to be "changeless."

Workable Words #45

"Stillness subdues stimulation"

Working These Words: There arc positives about stillness but there are also as well negatives and in the middle or center of life that we come to the negative sometimes greatly applies. Negative stillness can steal from us needed stimulation that is necessary for our new successes because it can silence stimulation. Stimulation is the provoking of self. We must come to a place in our lives where we make sure that we have positive stimulation to override the negative stillness in ourselves that causes us to standby and procrastinate or do nothing. When we provoke ourselves to a passionate degree for the positive we neutralize the negative and propel ourselves towards the positive. Therefore though negative stillness tries to suppress us or place us into an area where we will accept being still, silent, and suppressed positive stimulation activated within us will stir us up to think otherwise!

Workable Words #46

"Movement matures manifestation"

Working These Words: Movement is the ability to pass from one place of residence to another place of residence while manifestation is that readiness that we have for our own personal revelation. The middle realm of life can be used a birthing chamber for rich manifestation from our lives. However the degree that our manifestation is able to mature or develop richly is directly related to the degree that we have a readiness to move so that we may reside in a residence that will richly reward us. If we do not determine to move out of the middle then we may never see desirable manifestation. Determination to see desirable manifestation and to step beyond where we are will drive us towards a direction with beautiful satisfaction.

Workable Words #47

"Helpful viewpoints handles victimization"

Working These Words: Here is another helpful workable word that helps us to understand that helpful viewpoints can help us to handle the harshness of being a victim. Victimization deals with the hardcore realities of cruelty and many times with life in the middle we are confronted by harsh hardship that brings such cruel vexation. However helpful viewpoints in these times of being victimized can end up making us victorious. Helpful viewpoints bring us to see that we can be victors in spite of the hindrances that come about from victimization with its violations that violate us with the heaviness of hurt and harshness. A viewpoint that is helpful tells us that in spite of being hurt and treated harshly we do not have to be handicapped by this but we can transfer ourselves over to the hope of how valuable we truly still are!

Workable Words #48

"Capacity cures closure"

Working These Words: Closure always involves conclusions. Our situation with closure is always made solvable by capacity. Capacity is the present containment of certain particular contents. When opportunities in life appear to be completely closed we must open up the capacity of our output in a greater measure so that there will be a greater outburst of our output that will lead us to overpower all obstacles that obstruct us from opportunities and will eventually cause us to obtain these opportunities with all optimism. Capacity that is fully opened with its output can cure the obstruction that we face with closure that fearfully tells us that our future is brought to an overwhelmingly final conclusion but capacity instead tells us that the conclusion made about our future can be one of an ongoing opportunity to flourish!

Workable Words #49

"The grief stage comes before the grand stage"

Working These Words: Grief is involvement with gloominess and grievances. It is the stage of sadness that we at time stand upon. There is however a greater stage that we can also stand upon and it is a stage that can satisfy us with that which is grand. The grand involves that which is both great and glorious. The stage of grieving only prepares us for a greater, grander and more glorious stage to come. Therefore we should learn that as we release our grip on grief that gradually it allows us to grab hold of that which later on will be much more glorious and grander in scale. The releasing of our grip on grief today can lead to the rightful grasp for the triumphant in our tomorrows!

Workable Words #50

"Doubt deliverance brings desired permanence"

Working These Words: Doubt is disbelief and distrust and in the middle we must be delivered from the diabolical nature of this device. Deliverance involves the departure from discontentment and the depositing of ourselves into a developed destiny and when we are delivered from doubt we can bring ourselves over into that which both durable and desirable. Once we remove ourselves from the doubt which is passing we will reside in that which is preferentially much more permanent. Therefore our freedom from doubt will cause ourselves to be found in that which is decently fulfilling! There must then be a death and discontinuation of this devious device so that we are able to discover and come into the total dominion of our dreams!

Workable Words #51

"Patience purchases profitable productivity"

Working These Words: Patience is the manifested practice of perseverance or persistence and it can be used as a means for purchasing. The purchasing ability of patience is that in time it can purchase for us authentic productivity. Productivity is profit that brings about progression and we may also term it as progressive profitability. As we continually practice patience with its quality of persistence while we are in the central life we certainly and gradually will allow ourselves to qualify for that which can become most productive in our lives. Patience therefore over time can place us into that which promises to be profoundly pleasant!

Workable Words #52

"An unchanged voice cures unstable variations"

Working These Words: Here is something that needs to be incorporated into this in-between stage of our lives and it has to do with the substantial value of our voice. The unchanged value we place on our voice can be a reflection of our unwavering virtue to become unbreakable in the midst that which may attempt to make us unqualified, useless or even unfit. A variation can be a diversion or directional veering away from valuable victory. Instability virtually and even visibly is marked with the idea of a variation and such can attempt to indwell us internally on the inside! However one who does not change or remains unchanged in speaking of how confident they are on the inside in that they will not allow themselves to veer away from the virtue of the internal vision that they have for themselves will see variation being unsuccessful in having any victory over them!

Workable Words #53

"Defiance defies defeatism"

Working These Words: Defiance is an important word to note in our lives since it is a countermeasure against defeatism. Defiance is a form of disregard or disobedience. We must work ·the workability of defiance in the middle to work against defeat that is trying to wipe us away. It is with defiance that we disobey and disregard all of the dictates that defeat is trying dictate our lives with. Defiance makes a bold declaration that one will never be beaten by the badness or barriers that come with any defeat. It is this positive defiance that we are able to decide purposefully to drive through the devouring effects of every possible defeat.

Workable Words #54

"The exchanger is higher than the entertainer"

Working These Words: Here is an important workable word and it deals with exchanging versus entertaining. Exchanging has to do with the process of trading that which is of little excellence for that which is of greater excellence. Entertaining has to deal with engaging oneself in that which we have exalted. In the middle of life many times we entertain those items that we should actually be exchanging. Instead of entertaining that which may be infirmed and inferior we should look to exchange it for that which is exceptionally excellent because in the event of exchanging what is inferior for that which is exceptional we are involving ourselves in that which is effective rather than being entangled with that which is inappropriate for us since it impairs us.

Workable Words #55

"A soon focus produces a sure fighter"

Working These Words: Focus is the mental skill to be able to securely and selectively fix the facility of one's mind. To have a sure focus we must focus on that which is soon to come into our lives. When we focus on that which we have determined will soon come into our lives we develop at the same time a focus towards fighting for that which we are firmly sure we will be able to conquer! An unsure focus produces an unstable fighter. Thus one must be able to favorably apply or appropriate the mental skill of focus that secures one's mind in what one sees is about to arrive as their answer and in so doing one is be able to muster an attack against any aggressive force that wishes to cause one to continue to live in absence of their long awaited answer!

Workable Words #56

"Penetrate your negative by provoking yourself towards your new position"

Working These Words: There is a great weight of wealth we can glean from this workable word. Being provoked means being stirred up to produce. We are only able to penetrate the negative according the amount of provocation that we provoke ourselves with. When we provoke ourselves we are actually stirring ourselves up to produce those stable practices that will stabilize us for our new position. It is standing in those stable practices that will cause us to pull away from and part ways with that which is negatively perverse to us so that we can secure ourselves properly in our new position.

Workable Words #57

"An absolute decision acts against active disturbances"

Working These Words: This workable word speaks about an absolute decision. An absolute decision is a decision that acquires all of our attention and is able to act against all disturbances that may be active in our lives. The word absolute refers to wholehearted action. A decision that involves wholehearted action will wipe away those disturbances that may at present be worrisome to us. Such a decision will defeat the debilitating effects of any type of disturbance that essentially is trying to bring us into a place of decline through dysfunction! One with an absolute decision decides that they will therefore deliberately dedicate themselves to their accomplishments despite being disturbed by any type of agitation or obstruction.

Workable Words #58

"The space called blank can be the beginning of our stepping up"

Working These Words: The middle space of life can be a blank space which may be saturated with the blackness of boredom. However out of this saturated blank space can bloom for us the beauty of a supremely new beginning! Major boredom can indeed be a major feature of this blank space which is situated in life's middle space. We must therefore soundly utilize that which appears to be blank and saturate it with that which is brilliant so that it can become that which may be useful to us in a most beautiful way! The intention then for dealing with blank spaces is for one to intentionally infill the blank with the brilliant that then breaks one into an incredible beginning of betterment!

Workable Words #60

"A circle is always broken by a cut"

Working These Words: During the time that we are centered in this central area of life it can seem as though we are in a circle where it seems that we are continuously starting and stopping at the same central location. To escape a circle requires an exact cut. A cut in a circle is a slice into a shape that is continuous. Whenever we feel that life has become for us a circular motion we must creatively cut into this circle and thereby cut ourselves out of this misery of this motion by slicing through this continuous movement! The sharp cutting instrument of our self determination that determines to not be caught in any counteractive and contradictory cycle will sharply cut us through such so that we can have supreme conquest over such a cycle and carry or convey ourselves over into the correct direction for our lives!

Workable Words #61

"The freshness of fruitfulness flushes away our frustrations"

Working These Words: Frustration is a factor we must contend with in the middle especially when it at times may be meaninglessly, mercilessly and miserably forced upon us. We are able to flush away our frustrations with the activation of freshness that comes from fruitfulness. Frustration is a feeling of failure but fruitfulness is a function of that which is fertile. In times that we both sense and see frustration we should use it as soil and fully settle into that soil the seeds of that which is fresh so that those seeds will fully develop into a tree of fruitfulness producing that which is fertile in our lives. Frustration then can fail to flourish in our lives if we allow ourselves to go forward by being fertilized with freshness that is formed from fruitfulness instead of being fenced in with that which allows us to be frustrated!

Workable Words #62

"The dominant dominates their domain"

Working These Words: Here again is another workable word and it refers to the worth of two words which are domination and domain. Domination or dominating contains the concept of disciplined control over a domain or a district. In describing the middle life we most certainly can describe it as being in the midst of a domain and while we are in the middle we must become masters over the middle instead of allowing its mastery over us. Our determined mastery over the middle involves moving in the disciplined method of dedicating ourselves to controlling or taking dominion of life's middle domain. Using this method we are able to transform the middle and any mistakes that we may make there into a masterpiece.

Workable Words #63

"Continuation commands the complicated"

Working These Words: Continuation is the ability to carry on and in dealing with the concept of the complicated it is a critical aspect in being able to take command of that which apparently is complex. The complicated often involves a compacted or compounded obstacle. As we attach ourselves to the concept of applying continuation which we can call also our "carrying on ability" we will command all complexity because we will continue on till we arrive at a place of clarity amidst the cloud of confusion that centers itself upon us. With this "carrying on ability" we are able to carry on in clearing away all the layers of complexity that have been loaded upon us so that we will triumph with liberty over that which is complicated and when all these layers that are with the complex have been cleared away we will adopt a life that has cleaned itself from the cares that are tied to the complex.

Workable Words #64

"The hammer of hunger hammers away at our hard happenings"

Working These Words: Hard places always require a hard hammer to pound away at them. Hunger above which is more than having just a physical appetite can actually be that hammer to pound away at those rock-hard happenings that happen in our lives. A hammer is a hand tool that once successfully handled can strike against the hardness of those surfaces that have become hardened. The significant level of our hunger determines the significant strikes we are able to make against all the hardened or hardcore surfaces that belong to heavy situations. Hunger says that we will not succumb or bring ourselves into subjection to the sufferings of that which is hard but we will successfully hammer away at them till they become solvable!

Workable Words #65

"Substitution is better than being shortchanged"

Working These Words: Substitution is the ability to swap with that which we have previously selected for another selection which we now prefer as our preference. Being shortchanged however is opposite to substitution in that it involves shortage. In the circumstance of the central life we must correctly substitute that which has shortchanged us for that which will bring supply to us. Such a substitution must involve those elements that will bring us into a situation where we will excel instead of being in a situation where we are exhausted! When we replace our exhaustion that has eroded from us our encouragement and energies with that which is endurable and excellent we will rise above the erosions that come with exhaustion by virtue of our replacements that can emancipate from our exhaustion!

Workable Words #66

"Neutral does not mean nonexistence"

Working These Words: The word neutral may be noted as dealing with that which seems to be nonexistent and that which seems to be taking us to nowhere. In the essential makeup of the nature of the middle of life we can term such nature of the middle life as a neutral one where it may seem that our normal existence has entered into the norm of going nowhere. Though the general nature of being neutral in this middle zone effectively seems to nourish and nurture us with the news about our life just going nowhere this does not have to be the general norm! We can take the neutral and turn it around into a new norm where that which is nonproductive is no longer normal with us but only that which is noticeably noteworthy and to do this we must transplant newness into the neutral so that it is transformed from nothingness into that which is noble.

Workable Words #67

"Dryness is cured by dynamism"

Working These Words: Dryness involves desert-like conditions. In this dimension of life we can come into a dry environment where it seems we are being dragged through deadness that attempts to deaden and dry up every desire that we have. However there is a definite counteragent to counter the deadness that comes with dry conditions and it is dynamism. Dynamism is explosive desire that one has definitely experienced. Dynamism produces the moisture that is much needed to dispel or move dryness away. Once we allow it to work it will wet the worn out ground of dry desire and will work dry, depleted, discouraged desire into a dynamic ground that once again delivers its desired worth.

Workable Words #68

"The assembler assassinates apathy"

Working These Words: Assembling involves arrangement and one who assembles may be called an assembler or an arranger. What we assemble or arrange can become a weapon in our hands to assassinate the enemy called apathy which is conveniently found in the central life. In the middle life we must make sure that we assemble that which will become our warfare weaponry to war against apathy that makes its war against us. Our intentionally assembled weapon of war must be activated aggression. Apathy which is a feeling of disinterest intends to actively attack us so that we will not detach ourselves from it and activate our arising out of it. However once we have assembled our essential arsenal of activated aggression we will aggressively attack apathy so that it eventually becomes absent from our lives!

Workable Words #69

"The numbness of a moment cannot suppress the newness of the magnificent"

Working These Words: Numbness is dullness that produces a lack of liveliness and in the listlessness of the moment of the middle we tend to be numb or dull but such a lack cannot be allowed to cause us to lose that which might be magnificently born through us. The magnificent has to deal with that which is marvelous. The momentary obstruction of numbness that we may experience while we are in our moment with the middle of life must always be effectively overpowered by the notable essence of that which is essentially new and novel that moves us over into that which is marvelous. We must therefore realize that the temporary nature of numbness cannot be allowed to comprehensively triumph over the newness that the magnificent in all its majesty can bring and once we refuse to allow the nature of numbness to take over then we will allow that which is marvelously and magnificently new to thrive!

Workable Words #70

"Halfway does not mean helplessness"

Working These Words: In the central part of life we can end up in a place that appears to be a place where we only reach the halfway point. At this halfway place or halfway point it appears to us that we are just half of the way from reaching our ultimate aims and goals. However half of the way is not an indication that we are helpless or hopeless. Halfway simply suggests that there is still another half we are still yet supposed to have and it does not mean that we are handicapped but it does mean that there is more that we still can manage to yet still have that we are able to handle! If we have already skillfully and accurately managed to master the first half of the place that we are in then we can also manage to have mastery over the last half we are still yet to see success with because of the skills we have acquired in the first half. Thus being in a halfway position only means that we are midway from happiness and promotion.

The External or "Circumference" Life

Our External/Outside or Circumference Life is that part of our lives that is beyond the internal realm and is the exterior or seen picture of our lives that must carefully be safeguarded from corruptive elements so that we are able to capitalize on our external creativity!

Workable Words #71

"Right relations can deliver us from rough situations"

Working These Words: The relationships that possess that which is right can remove us from the pressure of rough situations as the above workable word puts forward to us! A relationship or relation is an association that applies relevance to our lives. However the rightness of a relation will determine its relevance to us in the time that is rough. Rightness in relations involves those whom we have given license to so that they may bring lasting and loving remedy, restoration, and repair. Once the relation we have deemed is right then we can have real remedy, restoration, and repair that will bring rest and relief and reformation to the rough dysfunction we are presently realizing which may have damaged us.

Workable Words #72

"Impartation/Input also determines importance"

Working These Words: Importance today is measured by one's output but according to the workable word above our importance is also determined by what we are willing to impart or input into another. Impartation involves the infilling of another with an investment. The greater the amount of our investments the greater there will be amplification of our importance. Therefore it is imperative that we instill into others our impartations so that we will be able to increase our importance! To the degree another receives the infilling of our wise investments to that degree will our importance be deepened both adequately and wonderfully!

Workable Words #73

"Firmness keeps us from falling face forward"

Working These Words: Firmness will keep us from falling face forward according to the workings of this wonderful workable word. The strong factor of firmness involves fixing oneself firmly in steadfastness. Steadfastness logically means that we learn to stay stable in the midst of struggle and thus we liberate ourselves from totally surrendering and succumbing to such. Firmness facilitates the fixing of stability in a secure fashion. Firmness is a strong factor that forces away failure that fabricates our fall because one's footing or foothold is fastened and fixed upon being able to stand in stableness. It is this essential factor that will enable us to enter into effectiveness and not enter into embarrassments, entanglements, ensnarements or even emptiness!

Workable Words #74

"A workable life begins with dismissing unworkable ways"

Working These Words: If one is to achieve a workable life it must first have its applied starting point in ridding ourselves from any ruin that can come about from shaky ways that cannot be readily worked into our lives. Unworkable ways are those ways that can lead to our undoing and eventually can make us completely undone. When we dismiss from ourselves these unworkable ways we will walk directly into that which will bring the ultimate into our lives. The weakness and waste of the unworkable once disposed of will determine the workings of winning in life and the unparalleled and unrivaled desire to be unstoppable.

Workable Words #75

"Powerful greatness is founded upon practical goodness"

Working These Words: Greatness that is wondrously powerful is always built upon goodness that is wholly practical according to this workable word. A great person is not someone alone who possesses the achievements of greatness but one who possesses the application of goodness. Goodness has to deal with being goodhearted and good natured and developing goodwill. The height of how goodhearted we are decides the health of our greatness. The gain of greatness results from the glow of goodness one is able to give. In other words if one is able to give the glow of goodness to someone who is in gloominess while causing them to glow with that goodness that one has given to them then this can gain for us great greatness as that person gives up their gloominess in exchange for the glow that comes from another.

Workable Words #76

"The having of enjoyment is not found in the having of everything"

Working These Words: For some having enjoyment means having everything but having enjoyment is rather having both ease and emancipation. One may have what one deems as everything but that does not mean that one has emancipation or ease. Emancipation concerns liberation while ease concerns lightness. Our encounters with that which is enjoyable must be evenly balanced with that which eventually brings emancipation as well as ease. Therefore in having that which is enjoyable there must be the having of that which brings equalization to our excitable enjoyments. We can have that which we have determined to be enjoyable but also ensure that having that which is enjoyable means that ease and emancipation is not taken away from us when we engross ourselves in that which we have deemed to bring us excitement!

Workable Words #77

"The march of happiness is always better than the moment of happiness"

Working These Words: Happiness for some is a moment but in its sensible reality should be considered like a march. A moment is a short time period whereas a march is step by step trek. Many people move only into moments of happiness whereas they should rather move into an ongoing march of happiness. One who moves into a victim mentality of unhappiness is one who is more than likely unknown to the merit found in the unbreakable marching forward in happiness because they have failed to turn a moment of happiness into an actual march. The march of happiness means we operate with true motivation where we are always motivated towards being happy in spite of that which may try to override us because we have made happiness our mission and when happiness becomes our mission then being happy will become truly meaningful!

Workable Words #78

"Assistance from one leads to the advancement of one"

Working These Words: Assistance may be defined as the act of aiding another and when we donate such to others it can help to directionally advance us further in the direction we are desirous of arriving at as long as we are willing to make these acts of assistance applicable to another individual. The more provision of assistance that we are able to provide the more positive application to our direction that we are able to directly apply towards our advancement. Assistance can be composed of creative actions that cause others to achieve. As we reliably assist others in the acquisition of their achievement and their advancement then they in turn shall reciprocate and assist us when it is required in the acquisition of our achievements which will lead to our adequate and acceptable advancement!

Workable Words #79

***

"Life is excitable, excite yourself with its life-giving excitement"

Working These Words: This workable word teaches us how to view life and that our vision of life's excitement determines the vitality we add to our life's essence! Excitement is energizing eagerness and enthusiasm! When we deal with excitement we speak not of empty excitement which can involve wasting or weakening our ways with that which is experimental but rather effective excitement which involves establishing our ways with that which energizes. That which effectively energizes us is found in entertaining excitement that is both life rewarding and life giving which tailors us with the exuberance and enthusiasm for living.

Workable Words #80

"An uncorrupted today leads to an unhindered tomorrow"

Working These Words: This protective workable word is worthy of heeding since it teaches us that how well we protect our todays will lead to how well we will have profitable free access to our tomorrows. To be uncorrupted means to be unmixed, uncontaminated, unsoiled, unspotted and unpolluted. Corruption can be like be the tearing of holes into the complete cloth of our tomorrow that can hinder us later on in taking hold of that which can be treasured by us in the time to come. However as long as we persistently live uncorrupted in our outside life we are able to position ourselves into the unrestrained, unimpeded, unbridled and unblocked access that we may have been looking for in our life on the outside.

Workable Words #81

"Singularity is better than duplicity"

Working These Words: There are two workable words that need to be further explained and these words are the words singularity which means to be definitely original and duplicity which means to be occupied with deceitfulfulness. When one prominently operates in singularity one operates with a singular personality but when one operates with duplicity one operates with a double or duplicate personality that produces deception or deceit from which disaster can simply be predicted. It is then dependent upon us to not have dual or double personalities which can bring our desires to the place where they will be both disappointed and also defeated because our duplicity has disqualified us from them being prominently developed.

Workable Words #82

"Extensions with boundaries balances extremes"

Working These Words: Extensions are stretching points in our external life that must have boundaries that will help stabilize us or balance us in the midst of being buckled down with extremes. The broad operation of the extreme has to do with the overextension and overreaching of ourselves beyond our limits. As long as we adequately know the limits of our stretching points we know how to amply stretch to the exact length without being adversely broken. Therefore balance in the extending of ourselves causes us to be brought into a beautiful environment in our external life where we ensure that we involve ourselves within our own borders and we do not create a breach or tear in them!

Workable Words #83

"Awareness distributed dismisses arrogance"

Working These Words: Arrogance is an attitude of aloofness and affects many though there are many that may not admit to it. When faced with the carelessness of arrogance there is a simple cure and it is found in careful awareness. Awareness is the ability to be awakened to that which one must activate their attention towards. To be carefully aware is to have the ability to be concerned adequately with the crises or afflictions of others! Once we operate with careful awareness of others we are able to cut down any attempts at being continuously arrogant because we will concern ourselves in the affairs of others and in so doing we are attracted to their concerns rather than being absorbed with the arrogance of our attitude!

Workable Words #84

"Our chosen pleasures reveal our clearly laid pathway"

Working These Words: From the above workable word it can be noted that the pleasures that we chose can reveal the pathway that will be clear to us and eventually cause us to prevail. Pleasure involves the pursuit of pleasing passion which can either be productive or perverse. Choosing perverse pleasurable passions can even cast us aside from a correctly chosen path that we may be presently pursuing while choosing productive pleasurable passions can protect us on our correctly chosen path that we are presently on. A correctly chosen pleasure also brings about a correct or proper path that can be clearly laid out before us to conduct ourselves upon!

Workable Words #85

"The changebringer converts the course of constancy"

Working These Words: In this external section of our life we either fall under two brackets in that we either are ultimately a bringer of change or enclosed and entrapped under the burden of constancy! Constancy as it is being explained here refers to that which is consistent and continual in its emphasis or in the course of events. Changebringers are noteworthy changers in the course of that which may be accepted as being normally constant. In the external life there is the normally constant course that one can accept as both essentially and completely natural in its character such as the course of events that involve negative circumstances. However the essential nature and character of a changebringer is to bring change to a certain course of negative circumstantial events so that it can be corrected efficiently and even be completely eradicated!

Workable Words #86

"An uninterrupted life is found in overcoming all upheavals"

Working These Words: If one wants to have an ultimate life that is without interruption it is found in not allowing oneself to become undermined by any upheaval. An upheaval tends to place us into an uncomfortable and unpleasant position because an upheaval occurs when there is an untimely uprooting. In other words in one moment when we may feel that our lives are firmly planted in another moment our lives can be forcibly pulled out from where we have firmly planted ourselves! To have an overcoming uninterrupted life however one must refuse to be upset or undone by occasional interruptions and instead of seeing them as impediments realize that they can be used to inspire us to have overwhelming intensity that can be harnessed as a tool to overpower these interruptions!

Workable Words #87

"Rejections done today produce damaging regrets tomorrow"

Working These Words: Rejection is the removal and robbery of our respectability. Rejection occurs as a regular ritual with those who are the rejecters of others. However those who are regularly hardened and hardhearted rejecters of others must come to the full and hard realization in that they may be harming and hurting their own future happy reality. The rejection that one rejects with today can bring us into that which may be terribly regrettable tomorrow. Rejection is more than only a refusal but it can obstruct us from future opportunities with the one who has been rejected because they may fail to receive us and choose not to operate with us any more when one day we may require their resources!

Workable Words #88

"Sincerity stalls senselessness"

Working These Words: Sincerity means the reliability of honesty and it is opposite of course to the harsh results of stupidity which can involve being headstrong and senseless. Senselessness is stopped or stalled by sincerity since those who situate themselves in that which is sincere situate themselves in that which is sensible at the same time. If we are seekers for sincerity then we shall seek out that which is sensible because that which is sensible contains the substance of that which is sincere within it! Thus we are able to squash any subjection that we may have of ourselves to that which is senseless only when we are willing to become seekers after sincerity which can school us in that which is sensible. In other words that which is reliable will be that which also is rational as well because the rational and reliable go together!

Workable Words #89

"Our scales set our satisfaction"

Working These Words: Satisfaction always at times seem to be our supreme search! However satisfaction is hinged to the scales that we have. A meaningful scale is one that has a series of standard measurements. In other words what we have as our meaningful standard of measurement for satisfaction will either move us over into that which will make us sufficient or that which will move us into shortage or a shortfall. Many are not meaningfully satisfied because the scales that they have used to measure their satisfaction many times brings them the manifestation of scarcity in satisfaction. Thus we must manufacture our scales in such a way so that the measurable satisfaction we want manifested will move us past what in mediocre and towards pleasing and promising sufficiency!

Workable Words #90

"Commonality does not mean longevity"

Working These Words: In the realm of lasting connections we often think that if we have common or shared aspects with another likeminded individual that this means that we have compatibility with them. However this is not always an indication that there will be long-term continuation with them. The core issue with longevity has to do not with merely compatibility but rather with competence for one can be compatible now but not measurably competent later on. Satisfactory competence involves satisfactorily containing those capabilities to continue to care for another. The external commonalities can be lost over time but that which is of excellent competence will cause the continuation of a connection to last!

Workable Words #91

"Preciousness is found in Pleasantness"

Working These Words: A person's preciousness is not found in how prolific they portray themselves to be or in the portfolio they carry or in the properties that they contain but rather in the pleasantness of their character. Preciousness refers to that which is prized and a truly prized person is one who is truly pleasant because one may not be able to present oneself as having a prestigious upbringing yet if one has pleasantness in spite of lacking an upbringing of prestige then one truly has the principle that can cause one to go up progressively and eventually end up living a life that has been powerfully uplifted.

Workable Words #92

"The upperpusher is superior to underpusher"

Working These Words: Here we see emphasis on two kinds of individuals that we can be that are found in the knowledge of the external aspect of our life. These two individuals are identified here are the upperpusher which are those individuals who push others up and the underpusher which are those individuals who push others under. In the external life we either fall in one of these two employments externally. To the degree that we employ ourselves in that which pushes or propels another upward to that degree will we be pushed or propelled upwards as well even by the very ones whom we have enabled to go upwards in their life also. Therefore those who largely cause others to progress are seen as those who later on will gain profitable prominence in the long run.

Workable Words #93

"Exaltation is embedded in enthronement"

Working These Words: Everyone in the external realm seeks to be exalted but encountering such exaltation is embedded in those whom we enthrone. Enthronement deals with establishment. We will either enthrone or establish those who will bring effectiveness to us or we will either enthrone or establish those who will bring ensnarement to us because those whom we enthrone can help determine if we will end up being worthily exalted. Therefore to receive exceptional exaltation we must be willing to entrust or enthrone or establish those who themselves exemplify those exercises that originate from an exceptional example so that we too can operate with an exceptional example as well!

Workable Words #94

"The privileged is not the possessor but the processor"

Working These Words: Those that are privileged are not necessarily those who possess much but those who are able in a necessary manner to process much. Processing involves adequately taking that which is in ones possession and producing it into that which can become practically applicable. A person of privilege is one who takes that which has been entrusted into their possession and processes it into that which can become a product of purpose which can be used towards the purposeful and practical profiting of a person! Possession is therefore not about the promotion of oneself as being "privileged" but rather the positive placement of others on a higher platform through the practical art of processing one's possession for positive application!

Workable Words #95

"Classifications are crushed by cultivations"

Working These Words: We face classifications from others who classify us callously and carelessly in order that they may contain us but these callous classifications can be easily crushed when we concern ourselves with the correct cultivation. Cultivation involves being concerned with crop creation. What we cultivate as our "crops" can cause us to conquer those callous classifications that try to corner us and crush us so that we can comprehensively be the champions over worthless classifications that attempt to work at cutting us down. Thus we grow, cultivate or create those "constructive crops" that are the opposite of those "callous crops" that others have tried to grow in our lives to such a degree that we can cancel out eventually those "crops" that belong to those callous and corrupt classifications that we have been categorized by.

Workable Words #96

"Profound significance is in sound difference"

Working These Words: Profound significance may be purposely described as presently seeing ourselves in a profoundly suitable manner. Such significance becomes only possible or probable and supremely and successfully purposeful only when we are able to possess and portray a sound difference. A sound difference is a sharp difference or distinction that distinguishes us from the rest of society. We are only definitely significant only when we soundly bring difference into society so that societal dealings are shifted from being substandard to being decisively and doubtlessly satisfactory!

Workable Words #97

"Our structure secures our stride"

Working These Words: Structure intelligently focuses upon the building of a supporting framework and this supporting framework is important in bringing security to our stride which deals with the steady or increased flow of our steps! Once we build a firm structure that is strong and solid we are able to have that stable support for our stride to function upon successfully! Thus the support system or supporting structure that we have in place is able to properly position our steps solidly upon the proper pathway that we have picked! This support system or supporting structure can be composed of a collection of those techniques and tools that will cause us to take our stride into a territory where there will be terrific satisfaction.

Workable Words #98

"Living partnerships results in a life-giving producer"

Working These Words: A living partnership is a life producer and the degree that we are able to draw from a partnership that is living to that degree will we be able to produce life. A living partnership is more or less in essence the essential "pairing" together of two or more individuals who are engaged in placing life-giving passion into each another. In the external realm the extent of one's partnership can energize one to reach a paramount position that can be par excellence! Once we have such lively "pairings" occurring then each participant in the partnership is able to benefit from the living principles of the partnership so that each participant or partner in the partnership becomes a life-giving producer themselves who will take the principles of the partnership and produce with those principles for the partnership a prominent payoff!

Workable Words #99

"Distinction designates decision determination"

Working These Words: Distinction is the discerning ability to distinguish or decipher difference. Decision determination is another word for decision making. The ability to decipher or discern difference will determine the destination of our decisions. This difference we are referring to is not the ability or the ambition to be different but rather it is the ability to know what is different! It is only when we know difference then we are able to knowledgeably tailor our decisions because we will designate our decisions in favor of a difference that is delightful or desirable or we will turn away our decisions from a difference that may be defective and defeat us! Thus in formulating decisions it must be founded up finding difference that either brings us into freedom or difference that either brings us into failure.

Workable Words #100

"Endings empties us of excesses"

Working These Words: Endings are just as good as beginnings and they can help extract out of us and empty us of every excess. Excess involves having extra and includes even having extravagance. An ending can bring termination to excess that may end up becoming troublesome. Excesses can involve being overwhelmed with baggage that eventually becomes a bondage which obstructs us. It is only when we call for an end to our excesses then we can exterminate all that which tries to enslave us so that we can enable ourselves to live an emancipated life. There is therefore empowerment that comes when excessiveness that can transform itself into extravagance comes to an eventual end!

Conclusion: You have now read these workable words but these words will yield its worth only when we as "workmen" and "workwomen" work them into our lives so that our lives can become a lives of worth! When our lives have been crafted with words of worth that work then we are also able to craft our lives into a worthy workmanship that also works! It is all dependent on us being a decisive doer so that based on what we do with these words will determine the drive that we have towards arriving at our desirable destinations!

For speaking engagements or for general comments on how this book has helped you please contact the author at the following email or phone number:

jurai4@rocketmail.com or 18686477562